SPONSORSHIP PAGE

THIS BOOK IS SPONSORED BY

....

....

AS A GIFT TO

....

....

ON THIS DAY

....

'Each one must give as he has decided in his heart,
not reluctantly or under compulsion,
for God loves a cheerful giver.'
(2 Corinthians 9:7, ESV)

BY PRAYER M. MADUEKE

PRAYERS TO PRAY DURING HONEYMOON

BOOK 9 OF 40 PRAYER GIANTS

© 2022 Prayer M. Madueke

ISBN: 979-8488733398

2nd Edition

Published by Prayer Publications.

This book and all other Prayer Publications books are available at Christian bookstores and distributors worldwide.

This book and all other Prayer Publications books may be purchased in bulk for educational, business, fundraising, or sales promotional use. For information, please email hello@theprayerpublications.com.

Reach us on the internet: www.theprayerpublications.com.

For Worldwide Distribution,
Printed in the United States of America.

III

FREE EBOOKS

In order to say a 'Thank You' for purchasing *Prayers to Pray during Honeymoon*, I offer these books to you in appreciation.

> **Click here or go to madueke.com/free-gift to download the eBooks now** <

MESSAGE FROM THE AUTHOR

PRAYER M. MADUEKE
CHRISTIAN AUTHOR

My name is Prayer Madueke, a spiritual warrior in the Lord's vineyard, an accomplished author, speaker, and expert on spiritual warfare and deliverance. I have published well over 100 books on every area of successful Christian living. I am an acclaimed family and relationship counselor with several titles dealing with critical areas in the lives of the children of God. I travel to several countries each year speaking and conducting deliverance sessions, breaking the yokes of demonic oppression and setting captives free.

It would be a delight to collaborate with you or your ministry in organized crusades, ceremonies, marriages and marriage seminars, special events, church ministration and fellowship for the advancement of God's kingdom here on earth.

You can find all my books on my website: madueke.com.

They have produced many testimonies and I want your testimony to be one too. God bless you.

CHRISTIAN COUNSELLING

We were created for a greater purpose than only survival and God wants us to live a full life.

If you need prayer or counselling, or if you have any other inquiries, please visit the counselling page on my website madueke.com/counselling to know when I will be available for a phone call.

EMAIL NEWSLETTER & ANNOUNCEMENTS

Never miss a message from me again! People who read my newsletters say that they have been one of the most important tools in their Christian walk. The best part is that a subscription is, and always will be, completely free. As a subscriber on my mailing list, you'll be the first to hear about my new book releases, be invited to my weekly prayer sessions, and get reminders about my blog posts and other helpful information.

To subscribe, please visit the newsletter page on my website madueke.com/newsletter.

DEDICATION

This book is dedicated to couples who are faithfully trusting God to reveal the purpose of marriage and family to them during their honeymoon. The Lord who sees your sincere dedication will answer your prayers Amen.

TABLE OF CONTENTS

ONE

THE MEANING OF HONEYMOON

Honeymoon originally denotes the period following a wedding. It is a vacation spent together by a newly married couple. Most couples view honeymoon as a period of harmony immediately after marriage. People believe that the first month of marriage is the sweetest. It is a period of unusual harmony following the establishment of a new relationship. The newly married couples often take a trip or vacation to enjoy their honeymoon.

And what man is there that hath betrothed a wife, and hath not taken her? Let him go and return unto his house, lest he die in the battle, and another man take her.

— DEUTERONOMY 20:7

When a man hath taken a new wife, he shall not go out to war, neither shall he be charged with any business: but he shall be free at home one year, and shall cheer up his wife which he hath taken.

— DEUTERONOMY 24:5

Let thy fountain be blessed: and rejoice with the wife of thy youth.

— PROVERB 5:18

In the scriptures, newly married men are permitted to take some time to stay with their wives. Moses exempted them from going to war for a period. In the Law of Moses, they are to be freed from every work. They are expected to be at home for one year in order to cheer up their wives. They are to stay back and rejoice with their wives.

However, in modern times, most people observe their honeymoon for a full month. Honeymoon should be a time to be committed to God, His Word and to each other. It is a time to reexamine yourselves to see whether both of you are in faith.

> Examine yourselves, whether ye be in the faith; prove your own selves. Know ye not your own selves, how that Jesus Christ is in you, except ye be reprobates?.
>
> — 2 CORINTHIANS 13:5

It is a time to review your past lives and tell yourselves the truth. It is a time to review all your activities from the beginning of the relationship until the wedding. It is also a time to reconcile how much money that was spent and how much that is available. This is the only way to know if you have incurred debts during your wedding. You also need to discuss with your partner how much both of you have in bank accounts. Honeymoon is the best time to discuss the future of your new family.

You can discuss domestic matters like styles or living standards and mode of expenditures.

You can also discuss family life like the direction the new family would take, education, employment, and size of the family. Discuss how to relate with extended family members as well and how to manage what both of you have.

TWO

HONEYMOON IS A TIME TO STUDY

It could not have been easy to study the bible alone. However, you have a companion now. Honeymoon is a time to evaluate each other's convictions about God's Word and your commitment to the Word of God.

As Christians, you should treat the bible as an authentic written Word of God. The Scriptures is to be preferred over your thoughts, dream, tradition, philosophy and doctrines. You must reject things that contradict God's Word.

Making the Word of God of none effect

through your tradition, which ye have delivered:

and many such like things do ye.

— MARK 7:13

For in that he died, he died unto sin once: but in that he liveth, he liveth unto God. But God be thanked, that ye were the servants of sin, but ye have obeyed from the heart that form of doctrine which was delivered you.

— ROMANS 6:10, 17

But he answered and said, It is written, Man shall not live by bread alone, but by every word that proceedeth out of the mouth of God.

— MATTHEW 4:4

Jesus died on the cross that He might pay the price of our sins. He resurrected and lives forever. Those who accept Him cannot be servants to sin any longer. You can use the period of your honeymoon to study God's Word, and practically deal with any sin in your lives. You must always live according to God's Word. His Word cannot fail.

Seek ye out of the book of the LORD, and read: no one of these shall fail, none shall want her mate: for my mouth it hath commanded, and his spirit it hath gathered them.

— ISAIAH 34:16

For the word of God is quick, and powerful, and sharper than any two-edged sword, piercing even to the dividing asunder of soul and spirit, and of the joints and marrow, and is a discerner of the thoughts and intents of the heart.

— HEBREW 4:12

Let the word of Christ dwell in you richly in all wisdom; teaching and admonishing one another in psalms and hymns and spiritual songs, singing with grace in your hearts to the Lord.

— COLOSSIANS 3:16

You have to believe God's Word and more importantly put them into practice. The air, water and other fast moving creatures may be quick and powerful, but the Word of God is quicker, more powerful, and sharper. It can enter the soul, spirit, joints and marrow. It heals, delivers, saves, sanctifies and empowers more than anything else empowers.

The Word of God is able to guide a husband and his wife to live in peace and harmony. It is rich in wisdom, and good for teaching or admonishing members of the family. There is no other book in which God revealed His mind other than His written Word. Intelligence, exposure and education would not be enough without the knowledge of the bible.

THREE

THE PRE-EMINENCE OF THE BIBLE

The bible is a book for every Christian family. Other books on earth can disappoint but not the bible. While emotional strains and stress could influence authors of other books, it could not influence the author of the bible. The author of the bible, the Almighty God, is omniscient and perfect. He cannot make mistake.

> For verily I say unto you, Till heaven and earth pass, one jot or one tittle shall in no wise pass from the law, till all be fulfilled.
>
> — MATTHEW 5:18

Forever, O LORD, thy word is settled in heaven.

— PSALMS 119:89)

The grass withereth, the flower fadeth: but the word of our God shall stand for ever.

— ISAIAH 40:8)

Stress does not affect God. He is eternal. He is the same yesterday, today and forever. Any form of disguise by men and women cannot deceive our God, the author of the bible.

At that time Abijah the son of Jeroboam fell sick. And Jeroboam said to his wife, Arise, I pray thee, and disguise thyself, that thou be not known to be the wife of Jeroboam; and get thee to Shiloh: behold, there is Ahijah the prophet, which told me that I should be king over this people. And take with thee ten loaves, and cracknels, and a cruse of honey, and go to him: he shall tell thee what shall become of the child. And Jeroboam's wife did so, and arose, and went to Shiloh, and came to the house of Ahijah. But Ahijah could not see; for his eyes were set by reason of his age. And the LORD said unto Ahijah, Behold, the wife of Jeroboam cometh to ask a thing of thee for her son; for he is sick: thus and thus shalt thou say unto her: for it shall be, when she cometh in, that she shall feign herself to be another woman. And it was so, when Ahijah heard the sound of her feet, as she came in at the door, that he said, Come in, thou wife of Jeroboam; why feignest thou thyself to be another? For I am sent to thee with heavy tidings.

— 1 KINGS 14:1-6

God knows the content of the human heart and other creatures that have hearts. He knows the beginning and the ending of everything in the universe.

Now when he was in Jerusalem at the Passover, in the feast day, many believed in his name, when they saw the miracles which he did. But Jesus did not commit himself unto them, because he knew all men, And needed not that any should testify of man: for he knew what was in man.

— JOHN 2:23-25

Since man cannot tell the future, we need God and His Word to guide us through our journey in marriage.

> Because to every purpose there is time and judgment, therefore the misery of man is great upon him. For he knoweth not that which shall be: for who can tell him when it shall be?.
>
> — ECCLESIASTES 8:6-7

> Remember the former things of old: for I am God, and there is none else; I am God, and there is none like me, Declaring the end from the beginning, and from ancient times the things that are not yet done, saying, My counsel shall stand, and I will do all my pleasure.
>
> — ISAIAH 46:9-10

One of the most beautiful things a newly wedded couple could do during their honeymoon is to pray, study God's Word and seek His blueprint for their marriage. It is only God's counsel that would stand. Therefore, you need His counsel. His Word reveals His counsel.

Men write books that reveal their thoughts, which is finite. However, the Scriptures are God's revelation of God's mind and will to humanity. The Word of God has solution to every problem in the universe.

> Heaven and earth shall pass away, but my words shall not pass away.
>
> — MATTHEW 24:35

> But the word of the Lord endureth for ever. And this is the word which by the gospel is preached unto you.
>
> — 1 PETER 1:25)

Likewise, you cannot compare heaven and earth with the Word of God. They will pass away but the Word of God will endure forever. God's original copy of the bible is in heaven and one jot or title shall in no way pass from the law, until all be fulfilled. In family and other matters, the Word of God is good for doctrine, reproof, correction, and instruction in righteousness. Husbands and wives, who wish to succeed in their marriages, must obey God's Word.

Persecutions, afflictions, which came unto me
at Antioch, at Iconium, at Lystra; what
persecutions I endured: but out of them all the
Lord delivered me. [17]That the man of God may
be perfect, throughly furnished unto all good
works.

— 2 TIMOTHY 3:11, 17)

For the prophecy came not in old time by the
will of man: but holy men of God spake as they
were moved by the Holy Ghost.

— 2 PETER 1:21

With the help of His Spirit, God inspired over forty different
writers to write the 66 books of the bible during a period of over
1,800 years. The bible is versatile and can meet the needs of
every race, nation, language and culture.

But he answered and said, It is written, Man
shall not live by bread alone, but by every word
that proceedeth out of the mouth of God.

— MATTHEW 4:4

FOUR

STUDY ABOUT MARRIAGE

When you have a rich father who died and left a will for you, you would wish to read your father's will to know his thoughts towards you. However, when you have no knowledge of your father's will, you may die without benefiting from your father's blessing.

A will is a legal declaration of a person's wishes regarding the disposal of his or her property or estate after death.

And this is the confidence that we have in him, that, if we ask any thing according to his will, he heareth us: And if we know that he hear us, whatsoever we ask, we know that we have the petitions that we desired of him.

— 1 JOHN 5: 14-15)

If you do not know God's will for your marriage, how would you know what His thoughts towards your marriage are? If you do not know that your father left one billion dollars for you in a particular bank, you will not bother to demand from such bank your inheritance. It is also possible you could live, suffer and die because of poverty when you have one billion dollars kept for you in the bank. Ignorance is a deadly disease.

How God anointed Jesus of Nazareth with the Holy Ghost and with power: who went about doing good, and healing all that were oppressed of the devil; for God was with him.

— ACTS 10:38

When he was come down from the mountain, great multitudes followed him. And, behold, there came a leper and worshipped him, saying, Lord, if thou wilt, thou canst make me clean. And Jesus put forth his hand, and touched him, saying, I will; be thou clean. And immediately his leprosy was cleansed.

— MATTHEW 8:1-3

A father's will grant you much power and right to get what the testator wrote concerning you. A will is a written document that backs you as God backed Jesus Christ when He started doing good and healing all that were possessed of the devil. Jesus Christ knew that God anointed Him with power. Therefore, He did not stop at knowledge alone. He went about enforcing His Father's will.

Well, you may argue that Jesus is God and He knows everything. Nevertheless, the truth is that you have the right to know God's will concerning your marriage also. They are written in the bible, therefore search for them. The leper who did not know God's will for his healing took a step of faith and asked if he had rights to receive healing and Jesus told him it was his right. Jesus cleansed him. However, other lepers, who did not make attempts in faith, died even though it was God's will to heal them.

> And the LORD will take away from thee all sickness, and will put none of the evil diseases of Egypt, which thou knowest, upon thee; but will lay them upon all them that hate thee.
>
> — DEUTERONOMY 7:15

Beloved, I wish above all things that thou

mayest prosper and be in health, even as thy

soul prospereth.

— 3 JOHN 2)

Thy kingdom come. Thy will be done in earth, as

it is in heaven.

— MATTHEW 6:10

It is not the will of God that sickness attacks you during your honeymoon. It is not God's will that you start your married life with disease. If you do not ask, you may not receive. God's written will for you is to be blessed and for your marriage to prosper. God's will for you is true prosperity, sound body, soul, and spirit. It is God's will for you to bring God's kingdom into your home. You can live in peace, prosperity and in abundance just as it is in your spirit. These should form basis of your prayer requests during your honeymoon.

And the inhabitant shall not say, I am sick: the

people that dwell therein shall be forgiven their

iniquity.

— ISAIAH 33:24)

> The thief cometh not, but for to steal, to kill, and to destroy: I am come that they might have life, and that they might have it more abundantly.
>
> — JOHN 10:10

People who do not know God's will for their marriage think that honeymoon is the best time to enjoy sex. Of course, sex is a big part of it, but over 21 percent of the time should be devoted to finding out what God wants you to know about each other; that is His will for both of you to end your honeymoon without traces of problems or iniquity.

He wants to forgive both of you all your sins. These include sins against God, against your fellow human beings, yourself and against each other. If you have to, tell yourselves what each other need to know. It is God's will to give you life in abundance, therefore do not end your honeymoon without exhausting every important discussion. God has made provisions in His Word concerning your new family. Therefore, do not miss it.

> For where a testament is, there must also of necessity be the death of the testator. For a

testament is of force after men are dead: otherwise it is of no strength at all while the testator liveth.

— HEBREWS 9:16-17

If you are born-again and a true child of God, then you have the power to enforce God's will as you wish, when it pleases you or suits your new family. Always remember that the written will of God for your marriage is in His Word. You have to be conversant with His commandments, promises and provisions, and claim them for your marriage.

FIVE

WHY DO WE MARRY?

This is the first question every intending couple needs to be acquainted with. You and your partner must understand the purpose of marriage. This is important because any family that negates the teachings of God or modifies it for its convenience would have much trouble and curses.

Great peace has they, which love thy law: and nothing shall offend them.

— PSALMS 119:165

[18]And the LORD God said, It is not good that the man should be alone; I will make him an help meet for him. [20]And Adam gave names to all

cattle, and to the fowl of the air, and to every
beast of the field; but for Adam there was not
found a helpmeet for him. ²²And the rib, which
the LORD God had taken from man, made he a
woman, and brought her unto the
man. ²⁴Therefore shall a man leave his father
and his mother, and shall cleave unto his wife:
and they shall be one flesh.

— GENESIS 2:18, 20, 22, 24

God declared that it was not good for you to be alone. Hence, regardless of any form of weakness that you would discover in your partner as your marriage progressed, you have to still agree with God that it is not good that you should be alone. You are not perfect, so is your partner. Therefore, the best you could do is to pray that God helps both of you to overlook whatever weaknesses you would come across in your marriage.

Adam gave names to all other creatures and they did not argue. Likewise, you can begin to give names to all your problems and send them to where they belong, not in your family. God's purpose for marriage is for you not to feel lonely.

And he answered and said unto them, Have ye
not read, that he which made them at the

beginning made them male and female, And said, For this cause shall a man leave father and mother, and shall cleave to his wife: and they twain shall be one flesh?.

— MATTHEW 19:4-5

But fornication, and all uncleanness, or covetousness, let it not be once named among you, as becometh saints.

— EPHESIANS 5:3

Your honeymoon should be between your partner and you. Therefore, pray that no strange woman, man or any creature interferes. Pray that you would remain one flesh. This is God's plan, purpose and provision from the beginning.

For the husband is the head of the wife, even as Christ is the head of the church: and he is the savior of the body.

— EPHESIANS 5:23

God's plan for marriage is to give a woman a head. A man without a wife is like a head without a body. God's purpose is to make a husband and a wife one indivisible entity. You need your wife and your wife needs you.

> Nevertheless, to avoid fornication, let every man have his own wife, and let every woman have her own husband. ⁹But if they cannot contain, let them marry: for it is better to marry than to burn. ¹⁰And unto the married I command, yet not I, but the Lord, Let not the wife depart from her husband: ¹¹But and if she depart, let her remain unmarried, or be reconciled to her husband: and let not the husband put away his wife.
>
> — 1 CORINTHIANS 7:2, 9-11

> His disciples say unto him, If the case of the man be so with his wife, it is not good to marry. But he said unto them, All men cannot receive this saying, save they to whom it is given.
>
> — MATTHEW 19:10-11

One of the reasons God instituted marriage was to preserve purity at home, community and the nation. It is not His will for people to commit sexual sins at will. That is the reason God made two of you to get married. He does not want you to go after other women or men in order to satisfy your sexual urge.

Your wife or husband is the only legal person permitted to have sex with you. This is because God wants to preserve purity and holiness in the church and communities. Never you have sex with any other person except your rightful partner. When you disobey this rule, you defy, pollute and contaminate not only your body, but also the church and the nation. God has not made any provision for sex outside marriage. Pray now that it will never happen in your family in Jesus name.

> For the husband is the head of the wife, even as Christ is the head of the church: and he is the savior of the body. [29]For no man ever yet hated his own flesh; but nourisheth and cherisheth it, even as the Lord the church: [30]For we are members of his body, of his flesh, and of his bones. [31]For this cause shall a man leave his father and mother, and shall be joined unto his wife, and they two shall be one flesh.
>
> — EPHESIANS 5:23, 29-31)

> Two are better than one; because they have a
> good reward for their labor. For if they fall, the
> one will lift up his fellow: but woe to him that is
> alone when he falleth; for he hath not another to
> help him up. Again, if two lie together, then they
> have heat: but how can one be warm alone?.
>
> — ECCLESIASTES 4:9-11

It is your duties to protect each other so that none would have any reason to search for pleasure or satisfaction elsewhere. Pray against the spirit of hatred, fighting, quarrelling, conflicts and hostility. Pray against intruders also. The purpose of marriage is to find completeness and fulfillment of living. You may not see the whole picture at once, but you and your partner would complement each other. God will use what is in your wife that is not in you to fill the vacuum, likewise you. If you give God a chance in your marriage, He would prove to you that He is a perfect matchmaker.

> So God created man in his own image, in the
> image of God created he him; male and female
> created he them. And God blessed them, and
> God said unto them, Be fruitful, and multiply,
> and replenish the earth, and subdue it: and have

dominion over the fish of the sea, and over the fowl of the air, and over every living thing that moveth upon the earth.

— GENESIS 1:27-28

And God blessed Noah and his sons, and said unto them, Be fruitful, and multiply, and replenish the earth.

— GENESIS 9:1

Thy wife shall be as a fruitful vine by the sides of thine house: thy children like olive plants round about thy table.

— PSALMS 128:3

Moreover, God instituted marriage for procreation. The institution of marriage is the primary place to rear children before they integrate into local communities. Procreation is fundamental to the stability and continuation of societies. That is why the main objective of any marriage relationship is to grow together in unity sharing your intellect, emotion, personality and spirituality.

THINGS TO STUDY DURING HONEYMOON

1. HUSBAND'S RESPONSIBILITY

It will be admirable to get a paper and pen before reading the following Scriptures. Doing so would give you the opportunity of writing your roles down as a husband and reminding yourself what you ought to do always in order to please God.

(*See* Ephesians 5:23-33, 1 Corinthians 11:3, 1 Timothy 3:4-5, Colossians 3:17-18, 14,1 Peter 3:4-7, John 13:1, 15:13, 11:36, 1 John 3:14-18, 1 Corinthians 13:4-7, Malachi 2:14-16, 3:16, Romans 7:2, Matthew 19:3-6).

Though the man is the head and has right to direct the affairs of his family, yet, he has no right to require of his wife or any member of his household anything that contradicts the will and Word of God.

> But Peter and John answered and said unto them, Whether it be right in the sight of God to hearken unto you more than unto God, judge ye.
>
> — ACTS 4:19

And kept back part of the price, his wife also being privy to it, and brought a certain part, and laid it at the apostles' feet. But Peter said, Ananias, why hath Satan filled thine heart to lie to the Holy Ghost, and to keep back part of the price of the land? Whiles it remained, was it not thine own? And after it was sold, was it not in thine own power? Why hast thou conceived this thing in thine heart? Thou hast not lied unto men, but unto God. And Ananias hearing these words fell down, and gave up the ghost: and great fear came on all them that heard these things. And the young men arose, wound him up, and carried him out, and buried him. And it was about the space of three hours after, when his wife, not knowing what was done, came in. And Peter answered unto her, Tell me whether ye sold the land for so much? And she said, Yea, for so much. Then Peter said unto her, How is it that ye have agreed together to tempt the Spirit of the Lord? Behold, the feet of them which have buried thy husband are at the door, and shall carry thee out.

— ACTS 5:2-9

Wherever God's authority is made of no effect, the husband's authority ceases. He has no right to require his wife to disobey God. A replica of Christ's love for His church is what God demands from husbands.

> Husbands, love your wives, even as Christ also loved the church, and gave himself for it; That he might sanctify and cleanse it with the washing of water by the word, That he might present it to himself a glorious church, not having spot, or wrinkle, or any such thing; but that it should be holy and without blemish. So ought men to love their wives as their own bodies. He that loveth his wife loveth himself. For no man ever yet hated his own flesh; but nourisheth and cherisheth it, even as the Lord the church: For we are members of his body, of his flesh, and of his bones. For this cause shall a man leave his father and mother, and shall be joined unto his wife, and they two shall be one flesh.
>
> — EPHESIANS 5:25-31

A husband is in no danger of loving his wife too much as long as he does not love her in greater quality than He loves God. Christ loved His church and died for her. If the need arises, the husband must be willing to deny himself, toil and bear trials in order to provide and care for his wife and defend her. Husbands must have the same care he has for himself for his wife. He should provide her needs, clothes and all her necessities. The greatest secrets of conjugal happiness are mutual love, kindness, loveliness and tenderness of character at home.

God expects a wife to respect and obey her husband, while the husband loves and cares for his wife. A true child of God would never beat or insult his wife no matter the situation. The husband remains the head of the wife until death, and the body cannot decide to be independent of the head and yet stay alive.

What a husband gets from his wife cannot motivate his love for her. Rather, it is God's command that a husband must love his wife. Christ displayed publicly His love for His church when he went to the cross and sacrificed himself. Husband's love for his wife is not complete until he is sacrifice like as Christ was.

> But God commendeth his love toward us, in
> that, while we were yet sinners, Christ died for
> us.

> — ROMANS 5:8

Loving your wife must be a sacrificial, unmerited and not conditional.

2. WIFE'S RESPONSIBILITY

It will be admirable to get a paper and pen before reading the following Scriptures. Doing so would give you the opportunity of writing your roles down as a wife and reminding yourself what you ought to do always in order to please God.

(*See* Ephesians 5:22-33, 1 Corinthians 14:34, Colossians 3:18, Titus 2:4-5, 1 Peter 3:1-6, Proverbs 31:10-31).

A wife's submission is not a favor to the husband. It is God's command. Therefore, she should submit in love, not as a slave. She should do it without grudge in her heart. She should love her husband with respect and treat him with honor and dignity. Sometimes, your husband may fail to meet up with his duties towards you. Nevertheless, that does not empower you to fail in your own duty towards him. Spiritually, a wife submits not unto the husband per se, but unto the Lord.

> But let it be the hidden man of the heart, in that
> which is not corruptible, even the ornament of a
> meek and quiet spirit, which is in the sight of

God of great price. For after this manner in the old time the holy women also, who trusted in God, adorned themselves, being in subjection unto their own husbands: Even as Sara obeyed Abraham, calling him lord: whose daughters ye are, as long as ye do well, and are not afraid with any amazement.

— 1 PETER 3:4-6

In the ancient times, great and holy women of God also submitted to their husbands. They believed that if they trusted God's Word and submitted, God would touch their husbands. They did it and it worked for them. God has not changed. If you submit to your husband as unto the Lord, you cannot regret doing so. Sarah did not obey Abraham because Abraham was good but because it was God's' commandment for wives to do so.

And he brought up Hadassah, that is, Esther, his uncle's daughter: for she had neither father nor mother, and the maid was fair and beautiful; whom Mordecai, when her father and mother were dead, took for his own daughter. So it came to pass, when the king's commandment

and his decree was heard, and when many
maidens were gathered together unto Shushan
the palace, to the custody of Hegai, that Esther
was brought also unto the king's house, to the
custody of Hegai, keeper of the women. And
the maiden pleased him, and she obtained
kindness of him; and he speedily gave her her
things for purification, with such things as
belonged to her, and seven maidens, which
were meet to be given her, out of the king's
house: and he preferred her and her maids unto
the best place of the house of the women.
Esther had not shewed her people nor her
kindred: for Mordecai had charged her that she
should not shew it. [17]And the king loved Esther
above all the women, and she obtained grace
and favor in his sight more than all the virgins;
so that he set the royal crown upon her head,
and made her queen instead of Vashti.

— ESTHER 2:7-10, 17

Now it came to pass on the third day, that
Esther put on her royal apparel, and stood in the
inner court of the king's house, over against the
king's house: and the king sat upon his royal

throne in the royal house, over against the gate of the house. And it was so, when the king saw Esther the queen standing in the court, that she obtained favor in his sight: and the king held out to Esther the golden sceptre that was in his hand. So, Esther drew near, and touched the top of the sceptre. Then said the king unto her, What wilt thou, queen Esther? And what is thy request? It shall be even given thee to the half of the kingdom. And Esther answered, If it seem good unto the king, let the king and Haman come this day unto the banquet that I have prepared for him.

— ESTHER 5:1-4

When you honor God's Word by fulfilling your part towards your husband, God's favor, grace and mercy would be your portion. When you have God's favor, He answers your prayers. God cannot turn you down in times of trouble. Your husband could be very wicked but with time as you perform your part on his behalf, God can touch his heart. When God does so, you would enjoy your honeymoon.

Esther's humility, meekness and good character made her to obtain favor from a heathen king. Her character announced her and made her to be preferred above others (*See* <u>Esther 7:1-6</u>, <u>2 Kings 4:8-10</u>, <u>Luke 2:19</u>, <u>Matthew 2:13-14</u>).

Esther was a woman of honor and very great. Her greatness was based on how she loved God, his prophets and her husband. She studied her husband and knew how and when to approach him. She was more spiritual and greater than her husband was but she respected him.

A good wife should emulate Esther. Even when she provides for her family, she would never publicize it. She takes care of her husband, her household and the people of God around her. She cannot do anything without her husband's permission.

A good wife is very industrious, spiritual and strong. She would not make a decision without obtaining her husband's permission respectfully. Mary, the mother of Jesus was never a talkative. She never boasted to her husband or disrespected him. An angel of God empowered her and the Holy Spirit overshadowed her to conceive the Savior of the whole world.

Nevertheless, these things did not make her proud. She submitted to her husband and kept these things in her heart. Other women would have made great noise, but not Mary.

When her husband planned to divorce her, she did not fight or argued with him. She did not go to court. She simply went to God and prayed as she pondered in her heart. That night, God sent an angel to talk to Joseph.

So many wives know how to prove things right before their husbands and talk in the court but they cannot talk to God. They can talk and get court judgments delivered in their favor. However, you cannot enjoy a man as a friend and a husband.

Mary was prayerful to the extent that angel of God made prayers on her behalf. If you emulate Mary's character, no matter how wicked your husband is, you can win him over. The reason is that God is able to send an angel to handle your husband.

But when Herod was dead, behold, an angel of the Lord appeareth in a dream to Joseph in Egypt, Saying, Arise, and take the young child and his mother, and go into the land of Israel: for they are dead which sought the young child's life. And he arose, and took the young child and his mother, and came into the land of Israel. But when he heard that Archelaus did reign in Judaea in the room of his father Herod, he was afraid to go thither: notwithstanding, being warned of God in a dream, he turned aside into the parts of Galilee.

— MATTHEW 2:19-22

Now his parents went to Jerusalem every year at the feast of the Passover. And when he was twelve years old, they went up to Jerusalem after the custom of the feast. And when they had fulfilled the days, as they returned, the child Jesus tarried behind in Jerusalem; and Joseph and his mother knew not of it. But they, supposing him to have been in the company, went a day's journey; and they sought him among their kinsfolk and acquaintance. And when they found him not, they turned back again to Jerusalem, seeking him. And it came to pass, that after three days they found him in the temple, sitting in the midst of the doctors, both hearing them, and asking them questions. And all that heard him were astonished at his understanding and answers. And when they saw him, they were amazed: and his mother said unto him, Son, why hast thou thus dealt with us? Behold, thy father and I have sought thee sorrowing.

— LUKE 2:41-48

If you are prayerful, Herod may seek to kill your children, but he would die while your children live. Your prayers will always bring down an angel to guide you through all your troubles.

There was in the days of Herod, the king of Judæa, a certain priest named Zacharias, of the course of Abia: and his wife was of the daughters of Aaron, and her name was Elisabeth. And they were both righteous before God, walking in all the commandments and ordinances of the Lord blameless. And they had no child, because that Elisabeth was barren, and they both were now well stricken in years. [23]And it came to pass, that, as soon as the days of his ministration were accomplished, he departed to his own house. [24]And after those days his wife Elisabeth conceived, and hid herself five months, saying, [25]Thus hath the Lord dealt with me in the days wherein he looked on me, to take away my reproach among men. [57]Now Elisabeth's full time came that she should be delivered; and she brought forth a son. [58]And her neighbors and her cousins heard how the Lord had shewed great mercy upon her; and they rejoiced with her. [59]And it came to pass, that on the eighth day they came to circumcise the child; and they called him Zacharias, after the name of his father. [60]And his mother answered and said, Not so; but he shall be called John. [61]And they said unto her, There is none of thy kindred that is called by this name. [62]And they made signs to his father, how he would have him called. [63]And he asked for a writing table, and wrote, saying, His name is John. And they marveled all. [64]And his mouth was opened immediately, and his tongue loosed, and he spake, and praised God.

— LUKE 1:5-7, 23-25, 57-64

If you are prayerful and remain righteous, no problem can break your marriage. Not even barrenness, lack, shame or reproach. Women who submit to their husbands as unto the Lord never bow because of problems. No matter how long challenges last, they remain candidates of miracles. The marriage of husband and wife, who obey God's command, will flourish until the end of their lives on earth.

QUALITIES OF A VIRTUOUS WIFE

- She is submissive (*See* 1 Timothy 2:11-14, 1 Peter 3:1, Colossians 3:18

- She is humble (*See* 1 Peter 3:3-4, 1 Timothy 2:9).

- She is reverent (*See* Ephesians 5:33,1 Peter 2:18-33, 3:5).

- She is obedience (*See* 1 Peter 3:1, Titus 2:5).

- She is hospitable (*See* Proverbs 31:20, 2 Kings 4:8-10, Hebrew 13:2; Acts 9:36, 16:14-15).

- She is meek (*See* 1 Peter 3:4, Esther 1:10-12).

- She is diligent (*See* Psalms 144:11-12, Proverbs 12:4, 1 Samuel 25:14-37, Proverbs 31:10-31).

- She is holy and loving (*See* Titus 2:4-5, Song of Solomon 8:6-7).

- She is a mother (Psalms 128:3, Deuteronomy 6:6-9, Proverbs 6:20-25).

- She is prayerful (*See* Esther 4:7-16, 2 Kings 4:18-37).

Luther once said of his wife, "*The greatest gift of God is a pious, amiable spouse, who fears God, loves her house, with which one can live in perfect confidence.*"

The founder of the Salvation Army, General Booth, also had a submissive wife. When he was still in the Wesleyan ministry, crises arose. He believed that God has called him to do the work of an evangelist. However, the Wesleyan conference voted against allowing him to devote fulltime to this work. It was indeed a huge crisis for William Booth. If refused to accept the ministry's decision, then he would leave the Wesleyan ministry. That means that he and his family would lose their source of livelihood, their home and fortune. However, in the midst of the crises, just at the point when Mr. Booth decided to yield to the decision of Wesleyan board, he heard a woman's voice in the gallery shouting, "*William, never!*" Behold, it was Mrs. Booth. She summoned much courage and urged William not to give in.

Instead of being very anxious and fearful of the consequences of resigning, she supported her husband. Her encouragement would later become the bedrock of Salvation Army.

At her funeral, her husband described her as "*A tree that had shadowed him from the burning sun, whose flowers had been the adornment and beauty of his life. A tree, whose fruits had been the stay of his existence and a counselor who had ever advised him and seldom advised him wrongly. A friend who had understood his very nature; a wife who for forty years had never given him real cause for grief, who had been the strongest when the battle was strongest. She was the delight of his eyes and the inspiration of his soul. She was a spiritual warrior.*"

One may say that a true Christian wife is to her husband and family what Shakespeare said sleep is to the body.

What testimony will your husband give if you pass away? Aristotle, the prince of Greek philosophy, said, *"If women be good, the half of the commonwealth may be happy where they are."*

I read about a woman whose husband did not hang up his clothes, as he should. This trait was sorely aggravating to the wife, who was neat and tidy, and she nagged him constantly in regard to it until she lost sight of the fact that her husband was a good provider, ambitious, gentle and kind at home, deeply spiritual, and an earnest worker in the God's service.

The scriptures did not say that we would go to hell fire if you do not hang up our clothes or if we do not know how to cook very well. However, all these are very important and can be learnt when you give your partner a chance. I also read of a man who nagged so much about his wife's inability to cook well that he became blind to see that his wife was a wonderful mother, an efficient home keeper, of sweet personality, a true and devoted mate.

J.R Miller said, *"The only thing that follows him around and refuses to be buried is the character of a man."* This is true.

WARFARE SECTION

PRAYERS DURING HONEYMOON

Bible references: Ephesians 5:31-33, Genesis 2:24; Malachi 2:14-16, 3:16; Romans 7:2, Matthew 19:3-6

Begin with praise and worship

End every step with prayers as you led

STEP 1

Father Lord, lead us and perfect Your will in our lives in our honeymoon, in the name of Jesus. Every enemy of our honeymoon, die, in the name of Jesus. Blood of Jesus, flow into our life and speak to us during our honeymoon, in the name of Jesus. Father Lord, direct Your angels to guide us in our honeymoon, in the name of Jesus. We dedicate our marriage fully to You, O Lord, through our honeymoon, in the name of Jesus. I cast out every unclean spirit that has joined us to this place, in the name of Jesus. Let every ghost of our past be frustrated, in the name of Jesus. Let any curse that was issued against us by any living or dead person expire, in the name of Jesus. Let the activities of our enemies be frustrated, in the name of Jesus. We break inherited bondages from our parents, in the name of Jesus. O Lord, arise and move this marriage forward, in the name of Jesus. Father Lord, give us Your divine program for this marriage, in the name of Jesus. O Lord, destroy anything that is contrary to Your will in this marriage, in the name of Jesus. Every plan of God for this marriage, begin to manifest, in the name of Jesus. Any power that was assigned to modify God's will for this marriage, die by fire, in the name of Jesus. Any evil personality that was assigned to frustrate this marriage, be disgraced, in the name of Jesus. O Lord, fulfill Your purpose and plans for our marriage forever, in the name of Jesus. Any evil sacrifice that was made over our marriage, expire by force, in the name of Jesus. Let every agent of separation, divorce and witchcraft in this marriage die, in the name of Jesus. Let evil spirits that resists progress, joy and peace in marriages be disgraced, in the name of Jesus.

STEP 2

I frustrate any evil personality that is attacking the love of God in my marriage, in the name of Jesus. Owners of evil loads in my marriage, appear and carry your loads, in the name of Jesus. O Lord, frustrate every Jezebel, Delilah and home breakers, in the name of Jesus. Any strongman that was assigned to destroy my marriage, fall down and die, in the name of Jesus. Let marital problems that are frustrating my marriage die, in the name of Jesus. Any power that was assigned to delay God's miracles in my marriage, die, in the name of Jesus. Let inherited covenant over this marriage break and expire, in the name of Jesus. Power of darkness that attacks marriages in dreams, my marriage is not your candidate, in the name of Jesus. I remove evil limitations that were placed over my marriage, in the name of Jesus. Let every evil program for this marriage be terminated forever, in the name of Jesus.

STEP 3

I command covenants with spirit beings to break, in the name of Jesus. Let every garment of shame and reproach in this marriage burn to ashes, in the name of Jesus. Every invitation that was given to evil spirit and satanic agents to my marriage, die, in the name of Jesus. I destroy every architect of conflict and hostility in my marriage, in the name of Jesus. Any evil personality that wants to redesign God's map for my marriage, die, in the name of Jesus. I cast out spirit of hatred that was planted in my marriage by home wreckers, in the name of Jesus. Let marriage breakers that are working against my marriage be exposed and disgraced, in the name of Jesus. Let evil imaginations, thoughts, plans, desires, decisions and expectations in my marriage die in the name of Jesus. Every weapon of barrenness, miscarriage and hardship that was formed against my marriage, catch fire, in the name of Jesus. O Lord, help me to occupy my rightful position in my marriage, in the name of Jesus. Let every problem that would arise in my marriage receive immediate solution, in the name of Jesus. Any evil counsel that was designed to overthrow my marriage, be rejected, in the name of Jesus. I frustrate interferences from demonic in-laws, in the name of Jesus. Let every work of devil before, during and after my marriage expire by force, in the name of Jesus.

STEP 4

Let every evil wish against my marriage be converted to blessings, in the name of Jesus. Any evil cage that was designed to cage this marriage, catch fire and burn to ashes, in the name of Jesus. Let the blessings of God capture every area of my marriage by fire, in the name of Jesus. Let any manipulator that was assigned to manipulate my marriage be manipulated, in the name of Jesus. O Lord, arise, destroy any spirit of sin, adultery, selfishness, lack of submission, and love in my marriage, in the name of Jesus. I withdraw my marriage from the list of marriage failures, in the name of Jesus. Let prosperity that will move my marriage forward appear by force, in the name of Jesus. Lord Jesus, reign as the prince of peace in my marriage, in the name of Jesus. Every good thing that would keep my marriage in peace, manifest, in the name of Jesus. Any property of devil that is bringing demons into my home, catch fire, in the name of Jesus. Let Jesus reign as the prince of peace in my marriage forever, in the name of Jesus. Any spirit wife, husband, children and evil relations in this marriage, die, in the name of Jesus.

THANK YOU!

I'd like to use this time to thank you for purchasing my books and helping my ministry and work. Any copy of my book you buy helps to fund my ministry and family, as well as offering much-needed inspiration to keep writing. My family and I are very thankful, and we take your assistance very seriously.

You have already accomplished so much, but I would appreciate an honest review of some of my books through the link below. This is critical since reviews reflect how much an author's work is respected.

Please visit https://www.amazon.com/review/create-review?asin=B09TH8QKVN or CLICK HERE TO LEAVE A REVIEW

Please be aware that I read and value all comments and reviews. You can always post a review even though you haven't finished the book yet, and then edit your reviews later.

Once again, here is the link:

Please visit https://www.amazon.com/review/create-review?asin=B09TH8QKVN or CLICK HERE TO LEAVE A REVIEW

Thank you so much as you spare a precious moment of your time and may God bless you and meet you at the very point of your need.

You can also send me an email to prayermadu@yahoo.com if you encounter any difficulty while writing your review.

OTHER BOOKS BY PRAYER MADUEKE

1. 100 Days Prayers to Wake Up Your Lazarus
2. 15 Deliverance Steps to Everlasting Life
3. 21/40 Nights of Decrees and Your Enemies Will Surrender
4. 35 Deliverance Steps to Everlasting Rest
5. 35 Special Dangerous Decrees
6. 40 Prayer Giants
7. Alone with God
8. Americans, May I Have Your Attention Please
9. Avoid Academic Defeats
10. Because You Are Living Abroad
11. Biafra of My Dream
12. Breaking Evil Yokes
13. Call to Renew Covenant
14. Command the Morning, Day and Night
15. Community Liberation and Solemn Assembly
16. Comprehensive Deliverance
17. Confront and Conquer Your Enemy
18. Contemporary Politicians' Prayers for Nation Building
19. Crossing the Hurdles
20. Dangerous Decrees to Destroy Your Destroyers (Series)
21. Dealing with Institutional Altars
22. Deliverance by Alpha and Omega

FREE EBOOKS

In order to say a 'Thank You' for purchasing *Prayers to Pray during Honeymoon*, I offer these books to you in appreciation.

> [Click here or go to madueke.com/free-gift to download the eBooks now](#) <

CHRISTIAN COUNSELLING

We were created for a greater purpose than only survival and God wants us to live a full life.

If you need prayer or counselling, or if you have any other inquiries, please visit the counselling page on my website madueke.com/counselling to know when I will be available for a phone call.

EMAIL NEWSLETTER & ANNOUNCEMENTS

Never miss a message from me again! People who read my newsletters say that they have been one of the most important tools in their Christian walk. The best part is that a subscription is, and always will be, completely free. As a subscriber on my mailing list, you'll be the first to hear about my new book releases, be invited to my weekly prayer sessions, and get reminders about my blog posts and other helpful information.

To subscribe, please visit the newsletter page on my website madueke.com/newsletter.

AN INVITATION TO BECOME A MINISTRY PARTNER

In response to several calls from readers of my books on how to collaborate with this ministry, we are grateful to provide our ministry's bank details.

Be assured that our continued prayers for you will be answered according to God's Word, and as you remain faithful by sowing seeds of faith, God will never forget your labors of love in Christ Jesus.

Send your Seeds to:

In Nigeria & Africa

Bank Name: **Access Bank**

Account Name: **Prayer Emancipation Missions**

Account Number: **0692638220**

In the United States & the rest of the World

Bank Name: **Bank of America**

Account Name: **Roseline C. Madueke**

Account Number: **483079070578**

You can also visit the donation page on my website to donate online: www.madueke.com/donate.